Jordan McAuley's
Celebrity Leverage Secrets

Jordan McAuley Interviews Susan Harrow On How To Get Booked On Oprah, In O Magazine, And On Oprah's Favorite Things

www.CelebrityLeverage.com
www.ContactAnyCelebrity.com

Now You Can
Contact Any Celebrity!

Activate Your Free 30-Day Membership To:

Contact Any Celebrity
www.ContactAnyCelebrity.com

Your #1 Source for Accurate Celebrity Contact Information

($30.00 Value!)

Activate Your Free 30-Day Online Membership:
www.contactanycelebrity.com/free

You'll get Instant Access to the Best Mailing Address,
Agent, Manager, Publicist, Production Company and Charitable Cause for Over 55,565
Celebrities and Public Figures Worldwide!

It's that easy!

You'll get Instant Access to all this and more:

Easy-To-Use Searchable Database
The Best Mailing Addresses For
Over 55,565 Celebrities Worldwide
Agent, Manager & Publicist Info
Celebrity Charitable Causes
Daily Real-Time Updates
Free Research Requests
Postage Refund Guarantee
Professional Tips & Advice
Toll-Free 24/7 Customer Service
Celebrity Gift Bag Opportunities
Plus much more!

Activate Your Free 30-Day Online Membership:
www.contactanycelebrity.com/free

Copyright Notices

Copyright © 2008 Mega Niche Media LLC

All rights reserved.

No part of this publication may be reproduced or transmitted in any form or by any means, mechanical or electronic, including photocopying and recording, or by any information storage and retrieval system, without written permission from the publisher. Requests for permission or further information should be addressed to Mega Niche Media LLC, 8721 Santa Monica Blvd. #431, Los Angeles, CA 90069.

Published by Mega Niche Media LLC
8721 Santa Monica Blvd. #431
Los Angeles, CA 90069-4507
Phone: 310-388-6084
Fax: 310-388-6084

Printed and bound in the United States of America.

ISBN-10: 1-60487-008-7
ISBN-13: 978-1-60487-008-4

Legal Notices

This product is in no way endorsed by Oprah Winfrey or Harpo, Inc.

While all attempts have been made to verify information provided in this publication, neither the author nor the Publisher assumes any responsibility for errors, omissions or contrary interpretation of the subject matter herein.

This publication is not intended for use as a source of legal or accounting advice. The Publisher wants to stress that the information contained herein may be subject to varying state and/or local laws or regulations. All users are advised to retain competent counsel to determine what state and/or local laws or regulations may apply to the user's particular business.

The purchaser or reader of this publication assumes responsibility for the use of these materials and information. Adherence to all applicable laws and regulations, both federal and state and local, governing professional licensing, business practices, advertising and all other aspects of doing business in the United States or any jurisdiction is the sole responsibility of the purchaser or reader. The author and Publisher assume no responsibility or liability whatsoever on the behalf of any purchaser or reader of these materials.

Any perceived slights of specific people or organizations are unintentional.

INTRODUCTION

Want to get booked as a guest on the Oprah Winfrey Show or appear in O Magazine?

Want to get your product chosen as one of Oprah's Favorite Things? Now you can!

Just think about the amazing exposure, connections, and other benefits you'll get from just one appearance on the world's number one talk show.

My name is Jordan McAuley, the Founder of Contact Any Celebrity (www.ContactAnyCelebrity.com). As part of my Celebrity Leverage Secrets program (www.CelebrityLeverage.com), I recently interviewed top media trainer and publicity coach Susan Harrow (www.OprahPRSecrets.com) about how to get booked on Oprah, appear in O Magazine, and have your product selected as one of Oprah's favorite things.

The tips Susan reveals in this interview will work for any talk show. So even if you don't think you can get booked on Oprah, they'll also work for Ellen, The View, Tyra, Martha, and more!

Susan reveals everything you need to know about how to successfully get booked on Oprah in this revealing, unedited, no-holds-barred interview including:

- The one thing you MUST DO if you want to get on Oprah
- **Exactly what steps you need to take to get on Oprah**
- Why the Oprah Winfrey Show is very different than other media
- **What makes an effective Oprah show guest**

- The #1 thing Oprah producers look for when booking guests
- **What Oprah likes – and does NOT like – to cover on her show**
- How to understand what Oprah's producers are looking for
- **The one thing you should NEVER do when speaking to an Oprah producer**
- Oprah's 4 hot buttons that peak her interest
- **How to find out exactly what show topics producers are working on**
- How to create a compelling angle for your product or story
- **How to get an Oprah producer to replace a previously booked guest with you**
- How to get in O Magazine and why it's different than the show
- **How to media train yourself at home**
- How to create interesting sound bites and talking points producers look for
- **What you MUST do when an Oprah producer calls**
- The best way to pitch yourself to Oprah producers
- **How to tailor your pitch to get the attention of an Oprah producer**
- How to be more visible and stand out over other Oprah guests
- **How to get valuable feedback from an Oprah producer**
- What happens behind the scenes when you get on Oprah
- **How to make the best of your appearance on Oprah**
- How to get your product selected for Oprah's Favorite Things
- **How to get invited back again and again**

GUEST EXPERT:

Susan Harrow

Harrow Communications

256 Center St.

San Rafael, CA 94901

415-256-8060 (Phone)

www.OprahPRSecrets.com

www.AppearOnOprah.com

www.AppearInOMagazine.com

Susan Harrow is a top marketing strategist and media coach who works extensively with Fortune500 CEOs, executives, successful entrepreneurs, and best-selling authors. Her clients include iVillage, PlanetRx, Pacific Bell Directory/The Yellow Pages (SBC), Bill Graham Presents, Gillette/Oral B, Yoga Journal, Design Within Reach (DWR), the North Face, Studer Group, Central Asia Institute, HarperCollins, and Random House.

She's the author of, "Sell Yourself Without Selling Your Soul: A Woman's Guide to Promoting Herself, Her Business, or Her Cause with Integrity & Spirit" (HarperCollins). She's also author of "The Ultimate Guide to Getting Booked on Oprah," and the upcoming "How You Can Get a 6-Figure Book Advance."

HOST:

Jordan McAuley

Contact Any Celebrity

8721 Santa Monica Blvd. #431

W. Hollywood, CA 90069-4507

310-691-5466 (Phone)

310-362-8771 (Fax)

www.ContactAnyCelebrity.com

www.CelebrityLeverage.com

jordan@contactanycelebrity.com

Jordan McAuley is the President of Contact Any Celebrity located in W. Hollywood, a service that helps businesses, nonprofits, authors, and the media get in touch with over 54,000 celebrities worldwide. He is the author of the best-selling "Celebrity Black Book," "Secrets to Contacting Celebrities" and the upcoming "Celebrity Leverage."

He's appeared on CNN and Sirius Satellite Radio and in national media such as USA Today, The Village Voice, Entrepreneur Magazine, and more. His services are also recommended in Timothy Ferriss' instant New York Times Best Seller "The 4-Hour Workweek," Dan Kennedy's "The Ultimate Marketing Plan," Dan Poynter's "Writing Nonfiction" and John Kremer's "1001 Ways to Marketing Your Books," which includes a chapter by Jordan on how to get celebrity book endorsements.

7

Jordan: Hello everybody, this is Jordan McAuley with www.ContactAnyCelebrity.com. Today I am very excited to be talking with Susan Harrow of Harrow Communications. She is the author of *The Ultimate Guide to Getting Booked on Oprah,* which you can find at www.AppearOnOprah.com. Susan is a master media coach and a marketing strategist who has coached and created successful media campaigns for people who have appeared on Oprah, 60 Minutes, Good Morning America, The Today Show and in Time, USA Today, People, O Magazine, The Wall Street Journal and The New York Times. Susan thanks for being with us today.

Susan: I am really happy to talk to your group.

Jordan: Great. Why don't you tell me about your background and why you started helping people get on Oprah?

Susan: I started helping people get on Oprah because my phone rings constantly. Every single week, I get emails from people who want one thing and that's to get on Oprah. People don't really understand what it takes to get on Oprah. Oprah is the crème-de-la-crème. It is the top of the TV heap so to speak. I created the book so that people would understand what it took and the necessary steps to be considered as a viable candidate for the show.

I have also taught at the Learning Annex. People usually say one of two things to me after the class:

1) Susan, thanks so much, I really appreciate the class and I am totally not ready or 2) Now I really understand what it takes to get ready and I am going to do everything in my power to get on Oprah.

Once you understand the process and how to accomplish moving through all of those steps, then you can decide for yourself whether you are willing to do those steps and whether you are ready. Does that make sense?

Jordan: It does. Were you a publicist before?

Susan: I was a publicist first. The reason why I became a media coach is I found was that I could get these really great placements for my clients. I got them on all the top TV shows, in magazines and in print, Wall Street Journal, New York Times, Time, all of that. Oftentimes once people were booked on those shows or interviewed by the media, they did not maximize that opportunity.

There are certain ways you need to speak to the media that addresses the needs of their particular audience while at the same time addressing the kind of people and business that you want to draw to yourself. I found with many of my clients they would get a feature in The Wall Street Journal but nothing happened with their business. I thought am I spinning my wheels really working hard to get people in these top magazines? What is the problem? The problem was them.

You can get on Oprah. You can get on Wall Street Journal, but if you are not saying the right things to draw the right kind of business and people in, it may not do you any good. Getting on Oprah or getting in O Magazine or anything is just the very first step of making your media matter. That is what I started concentrating on. Now, I media train people so once they get those great bookings, they can really maximize it and make the kind of business that they want happen.

Jordan: Many of the tips that you are going to be sharing with us today actually apply to pretty much anything.

Susan: They do. We talk specifically about Oprah because she is very different than any other media. **The most-important thing that people forget first is to be yourself.** Especially when you start looking at how did that person act on Oprah or maybe I should emulate them. What any TV producer and host is looking for most is:

- Are you natural?
- Are you credible?
- Are you likable?
- Do we believe you?
- Is your product or your service or your cause something that we can really get behind?
- Can you convey it in a manner that is compelling to our audience?

One of the things that makes an effective show on Oprah that they really love, can make their audience cry? Are you somebody who can tell a story in such a compelling way that you bring their audience to tears?

That is not typical for other shows in the industry, but it is typical for Oprah. On the other hand, too, you want to be able to make them laugh. **You do not want to leave people in that sad, crying state, but they want people who can move their audience, and every TV producer wants that.**

Jordan: It is interesting that you said how important it is to be yourself because that is something that you point out in your book, which is how Oprah became so successful.

Susan: It is.

Jordan: What is the story her manager told?

Susan: She was competing with Phil Donahue and they didn't think she had a chance. They said relax and be yourself. She said that was the best advice that she ever received. Oprah was not considered a "successful newscaster" because she would get emotional over the news. That turned out to be her strongest point because Oprah speaks her mind and speaks the truth. She is not afraid to cry and she is not afraid to express her emotions.

When you watch most TV newscasters you will notice that they have a very straight and plain face and they are not very expressive. I was watching Oprah the other day on a show about going green, how we all can preserve the environment and still get our laundry done. One of the things they suggested was a low-flow showerhead. Oprah says, "Girlfriend, you know, I can do everything else but I love my strong shower, and I am not gonna do that. That is the one thing I am not gonna do for the environment." She is honest and people really appreciate that.

If there is anything that I can convey to everybody listening out there is that we have too little honesty in the world today. The truth-tellers are the people we want as our leaders and who we look up to and who we aspire to be. Many people tell me that I am the anti-motivational coach because I tell the truth about what it takes to get on Oprah. I want you to know that this is what it takes to get a six-figure book advance. This is what it takes to get on Oprah. If you are willing to do it you can, but it takes that willingness and it takes a lot of hard work.

And just not anybody can do it that is a big lie. Not anybody can do it and obviously very few people do.

Jordan: What are some of the characteristics that you should have within yourself so that they think I can do it or maybe I shouldn't even try?

Susan: The first thing is passion and the willingness to know, because if I just discouraged you, you are not an Oprah candidate. Here's the thing. If you are passionate and are committed, you will find a way to get on Oprah eventually and through your experience.

The No. 1 thing that she is looking for in people is passion and expertise. It is the passion. If you watch her show, which of course I recommend everyone do, to become really familiar with the format and the flow and the style. What you will notice is that people are passionately committed to what they are doing and they don't care if they are on Oprah or not? Of course, they want to be on Oprah but they will continue to do whatever they are doing for the rest of their lives or however long it is right for them. It is what they truly believe in, and they are not going to stop because they did not get on Oprah. That is really the No. 1 thing, and that's what I see over and over again.

If you look at her guests, most of them, and certainly the people who are on regularly, are at the peak of their game. One of my clients is a peak performance psychologist, an expert. Yesterday as I was media coaching her we talked about the difference between top performers in any field, top athletes, it doesn't matter, is that they are passionate and committed to getting their goals and to being a top performer no matter what it takes.

Jordan: Do you find that people are trying to get on Oprah and they don't even watch the show?

Susan: Yes. That happens all the time. Yes.

Jordan: That something that you keep pointing out.

Susan: Yes.

Jordan: I noticed in your book you point this out over and over again, watch the show and be familiar with the topics and the things that Oprah likes to cover.

Susan: It would be very insulting for anybody to try to get on Oprah without watching her show. It is not doing your homework. Your homework is to be intimately familiar with any of the mediums that you want to be on and to understand and know as much about that person, particularly Oprah, because it is such a personal show.

Any kind of show that my clients are going to be on for media coaching, I watch that show continuously so I can be very familiar with the style, the flow, the format and the manner of that person. I can then perform as that host, so they get a sense of what it is like to really be on that show. Every show has a different flow and format in that way, and it is important to be prepared.

Jordan: If you ask most people, almost everybody is going to say, they have seen Oprah. A lot of people, especially men, would never say I watch Oprah every day, but that is really important if you really want to get on Oprah.

Susan: It is very important to do, and to know how much time you have. Typically on Oprah, 15 to 30 seconds, but it is more the 15 seconds. You have to be able to make meaning in 15 seconds and you have to be compelling. If you are not – and this is one of those media coaching tips, the person who is most fascinating will get the most airtime. The person who can convey the most information in the shortest amount of time, that is the person who the camera is going to love.

Jordan: What are some of the things that Oprah likes to cover or that Oprah wants in a good guest?

Susan: The first thing that she wants is that you fit into the angle of the show. You may be the top expert in your field, but if your ideas and your expertise are not angled for the show during that audition, you may not get picked for the show. It is very important to be able to understand what the Oprah producers are looking for before you even open your mouth.

One of the things that you can ask is tell me a little bit about the angle that you are looking for, so then you can gear your answers to what they want. Before you even open your mouth you would talk about that.

One of the big no-no's in any kind of conversation with an Oprah producer is you are never trying to pitch your product, your service, your book or your cause. What you are doing is you are proving to that producer that you are the right expert for the show they are looking to create. That you bring that talent and talkability, that you are mediagenic. You are also someone who is really engaging and who the audience is going to pay attention to. Is that what you were looking for, Jordan? Did I answer your question or were you looking for something else?

Jordan: You did. You answered my question. Just to continue, you talk about Oprah's hot buttons. I don't know if you want to talk about them or do you want me to go through each one? I think you have four.

Susan: Yes, I do have four. I pulled them up in front of me so I can remember because memory is not one of my strong points. This is something that you can do also for a producer. I said, Jordan, can you walk me through those points? If you bring up the point I can talk about it because I may not remember all of those points. You say, okay. You have these four great points, and you can also talk to a producer and say, I have four points. Can you walk me through it? You mention the first point and I will take it from there. These are things that you can do once you are booked on the show. You don't do that in an audition interview.

Jordan: Okay.

Susan: Thank you, Jordan. I appreciate that. So Oprah's four hot buttons:

1. **Her motto is take charge.** That is consistent through Oprah and her life is to take responsibility for your own life and to live your best life. If you are doing that on a daily basis then that is something that Oprah is interested in. You are not only committed to your work but you are living it in a daily manner.

I love what Gandhi said, "I am the message to the world." Everything that you do, say and are is in complete alignment with what you are promoting.

2. **Personal choice**. Most people, Oprah says, are directed by voices outside of themselves, whether it is your parents or your work or whatever. **Personal choice is about making your own way in the world and really following your own voice to be the person you want to be in this world.** I was just listening to Anne LaMott, who is a fabulous author and speaker. She wrote *Bird by Bird*, one of my favorite books for writers. What everybody loved so much about Anne LaMott, who has a huge following, is that she tells the ugly truth but she is hilarious about it.

She was telling a story about how she helped kill one of her best friends. It was a very hard story to listen to, but at the same time very beautiful, very moving and very honest. Very few people are willing to do that kind of thing.

She gets lots of hate mail. She just wrote a letter about slapping her son, who was in his teens, and she wasn't proud of that but she wrote it. She got hate mail about what a horrible person she is. That is the kind of thing that Oprah looks for.

3. **Child and domestic abuse**. Oprah is still completely committed to fight against the abuse of women and children. It is not just preventing that abuse, but improving the lives of women in some way, shape or form, particularly women and children.

4. **Education.** Education changed everything for Oprah. She also wants to change education and help women and children become educated, like what she is doing in Africa. If you will notice that this year, there is really a focus on people who are making major change in the world, outside the political system. That is really a trend in our society today.

We have rogue people who no matter what the political system is they are following their mission and making a difference in this and other countries in their own way without the support of the government or necessarily the government of those countries. That is pretty miraculous in our country. Oprah is finding a lot of those people. It is a testament to her that she is so committed to inspiring all of us through these remarkable acts of both ordinary people and people who are ordinary people who become extraordinary.

Jordan: And it seems to me that for the people listening to the call that may have products or a book or a business, the first hot button take charge might be the easiest to focus on. Many times Oprah will have a show about a stay-at-home mom that started her own business to make extra money for her kids and it exploded into a worldwide brand. A lot of people really wouldn't be able to focus on child and domestic abuse.

Susan: These are her hot buttons meaning these are the broader issues that she has spoken on. Everybody can go to www.Oprah.com to see what the shows are that she is looking for people right now. You can take a look there and say, do I fit into something that they are interested in doing at this time? Those are more specific kinds of things. These are very broad.

For example, she just had a show as I mentioned, on going green. That would notfit into these categories, but it does fit into **educating the public**. It is not educating girls, necessarily, but it is. It is starting with the mom and saying if you want to run your household and keep your kids healthy you can go green. Here is how it is going to affect you in all different ways.

One of the people that she had on was a mom with a kid who was real young, 1) or 2) He was coughing and getting asthma. They could not figure it out. It turned out it was because of these household products that they were using. She went on this process of investigating so she could change these products for her son. If you can see that this big issue really boiled down to a small issue was she wanted to keep her children healthy.

Jordan: I was thinking more of creating an angle for your pitch. Later we will talk about how to get the producers interested in your pitch. What are some of the topics Oprah does not cover or does not like to cover?

Susan: She does not cover psychics. I know a lot of psychics want to be on the show. She did not really cover sex and sex topics, but she does now. She has asked the things like, is your husband gay? Or are you gay? Or have you been living a lie in your life? She addresses these kind of domestic issues that may look more salacious. What she finds is that there are a lot of people with these kind of hidden lies and she is bringing that to the surface. I am not sure what the other ones that she doesn't cover that you are looking for, Jordan. If you could guide me on that, did you have a specific idea of things?

Many people still ask me about her book club. For the most part, she has only chosen a couple of living authors for her book club right now and those are her fiction books. For some non-fiction too, obviously Elie Wiesel and who was the guy, James Frey?

Jordan: Oh yes.

Susan: That is not something that they are actively looking for. It is more about what happens in a smaller groundswell within Oprah's producers or has been brought to Oprah's attention, usually by a friend. If you have a non-fiction book, meaning you are an expert in something, that's fine, but it is not the book that is getting promoted, it is that are an expert on the topic you are covering in the book.

Jordan: For a while, she had a big celebrity almost every day. That seems it has toned down a little bit.

Susan: She has moved more into the political realm right now, more toward the political and the social. For all of you on the call, she is very interested right now in the way that our country is being led and how citizens are really making a difference on their own in spite of the way that the government is going.

The other thing that she is really focusing on is people who have charities or missions in their life where they really are impacting a huge number of people. One of the people who she had on the show we interviewed for O Magazine, first she was in O Magazine, Genevieve Piturro. She created The Pajama Program. When she was starting to do volunteer work, before she created her own non-profit, she noticed that when she was reading to kids before they went to bed she said, "Aren't you going to change into your pajamas?" She remembers one kid saying, what are you talking about? What are those?

When she thought these kids were going to bed without their pajamas on she became committed to getting them pajamas so they could change into fresh, cozy pajamas and go to sleep with a good bedtime story and cozy pajamas. Many of these children come from abused homes and, and their mothers were in prison. She was first in O Magazine and then she was on the Oprah show. It was pretty amazing because the way the show went is that Oprah had let the audience know there was a challenge for them to get as many pajamas as they could.

One woman got 32,000 pajamas and they rolled them out in these big laundry baskets that you see in hotels onto the stage. She was committed to doing this and then Oprah got the whole audience involved. The audience raised about half as many pajamas as she had for the whole time that her organization had been in place. Oprah is asking citizens to start taking a role in helping other people who have established these charities or non-profits or visions. She is getting her audience and other people all over the world involved in this. It appears that this one of her focuses this year.

Jordan: What you are saying is there are cycles of themes?

Susan: Yes, there are. There are trends and themes. This is one of the themes and trends that I have observed for this year that is pretty consistent. She is also focusing on health a lot with Dr. Oz, and your personal health. She has had a lot of shows with him and specifics. There is a lot of opportunity for health professionals out there and for people who are doing projects that make a difference to a mass number of people.

Jordan: This is one of the reasons that it is important to watch Oprah every day, and with TiVo there is not really an excuse.

Susan: That's right.

Jordan: If you watch it every day and someone starts to see a theme and they think this fits in perfectly with what I'm doing, do you really have time to pitch and get on the show? Or by the time you start working on it, has the next theme started?

Susan: Not necessarily. Sometimes Oprah goes on a jag. What they are interested in is creating a really great show. If there is a theme that is popular and she really does pay attention to the mail and how much response she gets, she may continue.

When you take a look on the Oprah site and see which shows are upcoming, just because the show was slated and you think, "That is my area of expertise, I wish I would have gotten in on the action." You can. Unfortunately or fortunately, depending on which side you're on, Oprah's producers and every producer in the business wants the best guest possible. If you happen to be a better guest than somebody that they have already slated, they will boot them. It is a sad fact, but it is the truth. As long as you understand that this is the way the world works and you can be on both sides of the coin that is the way things are.

It is up to you to say, here is why I should be on this show, and they may not boot somebody off. They may just include you in the show. The show can also shift because if you have a perspective that suddenly is more interesting than the original show that they were planning, they will shift. Things shift at the very last minute.

One of my clients who I had media coached, to be on the Oprah show, she had already been on twice and she had not had much of an impact. She hired me because she said, "I really want to sell my book and products on this show and I'm not doing something right. I have been on twice and it hasn't worked out." We media coached her to be able to be compelling, interesting, warm and wonderful enough that people would want to buy those products. We had worked very hard on her sound bytes. She called me on a Saturday and said, "We have been taping for 14 hours a day over the whole weekend. She said they are changing the focus of the show. Please help.

Know that the show's focus can change in the middle of taping the angle and the direction can change. Imagine the kind of skills and resiliency that you need to have, first of all, to be able to work 14-hour days, in this particular case, and then to be resilient enough to go with the flow and be able to rework your sound bytes on the spot.

Jordan: Before we go into the nitty-gritty technical things of pitching, I wanted you to talk about your book offer.

Susan: I have two books that go hand in hand: *The Ultimate Guide to Getting Booked on Oprah* and it's not just the book, it is the whole kit. It is CD's, the online version and the hardcopy version that really tells you the ten steps to what it takes to getting on her show. I have covered each of those very thoroughly, and we are giving you a lot of information today. Obviously I can't cover everything that is in that couple of hundred pages.

It really gives you a step-by-step process to do that, and then we are combining that with *How to Get in O Magazine*, because there is a synergy between the two. You may get in the magazine first then get on the show or vice-versa. There is a synergy that happens between the two and to understand again what it takes to get a product. **O Magazine is more product-focused than the show and the articles are more in depth than the show can go on a particular subject.** These two things *Get into O Magazine* and the Oprah Kit we are selling together today for $100.00 off. Instead of $344.00, we are selling it for $244.00. You can get the special, at this URL, www.snipurl.com/1i4an. Some of you are thinking that $244.00 is quite a lot of money. I do understand that people are on a budget and that information is not information that you can get anywhere else. It is very specific to Oprah. I wanted you to have both of these products because it is important to understand how things work behind the scenes. If you think about that kind of investment for being on a show and selling hundreds of thousands of dollars of products or services, and the exposure and connections that you can get from that kind of appearance, then ask yourself if it is worth $244.00.

Jordan: I will email that link to everyone that registered for the call. If for some reason you thought it was complicated, check your email and you should find it there. The $100.00 off is good for the next two days.

Susan: Yes, it ends at midnight.

Jordan: Friday at midnight?

Susan: Friday at midnight, Eastern Time on the 27th of April.

Jordan: Only until Friday at midnight you get $100.00 off, $244.00 instead of $344.00. It is for the Oprah Kit and the O Magazine book, which is really good. I was reading it last night.

Susan: Oh great.

Jordan: We will go over that in a few minutes. If you happen to hear this later, because we post these in the members area or if you hear it on a CD, and the special is over, you can go to www.AppearOnOprah.com and find the same products. You just won't get the special discount. Is it easier to get in O Magazine than on the show?

Susan: I wouldn't say it is easier. It is a little bit of a different process. The great thing about the magazine is that people keep it around the house and it is not the kind of magazine that people throw away. People keep that magazine and sales can continue for a very long time whereas TV is more quick when people are thinking about it, watching it, they act right then and then they forget about it.

The one thing to know about the magazine is it is the same high quality as the show. To get into the magazine your products, your service, or your cause have to be packaged very beautifully and very professionally. One of the publicists that I had interviewed for O Magazine said she had a fabulous client with a fabulous product, but she was not going to submit it because the packaging was not up to snuff and she knew that Oprah's magazine would not accept it. That is on the product side of things. If there is a story with your product, meaning you have a great story about how this product came to be, you are a fascinating person and that can be all encapsulated into how the product came to be, that is of interest to Oprah too versus just featuring a product.

For the other areas of Oprah, meaning if you want to get profiled or featured in the magazine, you have to be somebody that is doing something very dramatic in the culture right now in order to be profiled for the magazine. That means you are impacting many people in a profound way. Oprah looks for people who already have a following.

Jordan: If someone wants to be on Oprah, do they need to have prior television experience?

Susan: Yes absolutely. Getting on Oprah is like trying to run a marathon without walking a mile. There are so many things to consider to being on Oprah. You have to be so fluid in your kind of conversation and to understand and be able to speak about your subject with ease when there are bright lights on you. There are millions of people looking at you and things are changing at the last minute. It is really frantic. To be able to maintain your composure, and say what you are going to say in a compelling fashion, while it is in the middle of a conversation, because typically you're not the only one on the show. It is more like being in the midst of an Italian family where everybody is talking at once, and then they say, okay, Jordan, what do you think? And you are like, uh.

You have to be very used to that kind of ping-pong conversation and that takes an enormous amount of practice.

Jordan: And obviously, not being star struck. I watch the show and I think how do people talk to Oprah like she is their best friend without being a little intimidated to talk to her. Does she come out when you get booked on the show and introduce herself or talk to you before or is that the first time you see her?

Susan: No, typically you meet her when you are on the set. You are in the green room with other people, or you are in the green room by yourself and five, four, three, two, one, you walk out, you know, you are on the show or they cut to a commercial and you are sitting in the seat and badda-bing, there you are.

It makes me nervous looking at it and just thinking about it. I did TV for my media tour, and have done a lot of media coaching before that.

I have not done a lot of TV on my own, so it was really a great experience when I was touring for *Sell Yourself Without Selling Your Soul* to really understand it. Sitting in the green room, thinking, "Oh my god I am going to be on a show for two minutes", and it goes by so fast. You can't even believe it. It is like a blink of an eye for those two or four minutes. Even if it is a show that lasts an hour with commercials it is 45 minutes.

Your total time is usually about two minutes of talk time. You have to express yourself compellingly in those two minutes. If it is a more lengthy show, it may be 15 minutes total with the back and forth kind of conversation. You have to be ready with sound bytes in a compelling way and be very fluid and comfortable with your material so you can think on your feet. Have the sound bytes prepared because the whole point of media coaching is to become fluid. It is to become so prepared that you are free to be spontaneous. You know your material and understand the subject so well that when it is something that you have never talked about before you can speak naturally.

Jordan: What are some tips for creating sound bytes? In your book, you talk about how important it is to be blurb-able, and to have sound bytes.

Susan: **Sound bytes can be expandable and collapsible from 10 seconds to 30 seconds.** They are everything from anecdotes to one-liners to stories. Particularly for Oprah, you want to talk about stories because that is what really works on Oprah. Genevieve Piturro when she was on told the story of how she was riding on the subway and knew she wanted more meaning in her life. She decided that she needed to start this charity for these kids. Her publicist created a very compelling pitch, which I am going to find and read to you because it was really lovely. Oftentimes these sound bytes are simple but they convey a lot with very little words, does that make sense?

Jordan: Yes it does. Is there a difference between talking points and sound bytes? Can you explain?

Susan: There is really no difference. It is saying the same thing. You want to have stories and things ready because of the pressure that happens when you are on the show. If those stories are not hard wired in your brain, then when you are nervous, Cortisol gets into that brain and zaps out those thoughts. You may think you know some things but when you are under pressure and nervous and all these things going on and you haven't rehearsed it enough, then you don't remember it. You are caught like a deer in the headlights.

Let me read what their pitch was for this particular show. "When you were a child did you go to bed naked or wear your street clothes as pajamas? For many under privileged youngsters that is a way of life. Genevieve Piturro, Executive Director and Founder of The Pajama Program is working to change that." It moves on from there. That kind of headline is very important in your pitch and can also be used as a sound byte.

Genevieve Piturro said, when she was tucking these children in they were in their street clothes and she was just completely struck by that. We are living in America, the richest country in the world and kids are going to bed in street clothes or naked. What kind of world is this? I want to change that. That is an example of a sound byte. It is can be a very short story that takes about ten seconds to tell. You want to have stories with emotional resonance that are compelling to an audience that can be very quickly conveyed. They may also be statistics, what percentage of the population is suffering from this particular disease or ailment or psychological disorder and be able to mix that in. You have:

- Statistics
- Emotional stories
- Things about your personal life
- Things about your professional life
- How you have impacted people

Jordan: What if you don't have a charity or a non-profit? How can you get the attention of a producer if you have something else and want to get on the show?

Susan: It is all about the angle. It is all about what is going on in the culture today that is important to Oprah's audience. It doesn't have to be a charity. That is one of the things I am focusing on because she is focusing on that a lot on the show.

For example, one of my clients was severely abused when she was a child and speaks out on that. She is an expert in grief counseling. Oprah's producers called her after the Virginia Tech massacre and said, "Could you come on the show with students from Virginia Tech and talk about releasing grief? She was an expert in moving through grief.

It is about being an expert on a particular topic that happens to be topical today.

You can:

- Speak to us
- Educate us
- Enlighten us in some way that is of interest.

These topics include how to prevent identity theft scams to other things that are happening in the culture today.

Jordan: How important is it to have a book to be considered an expert for Oprah?

Susan: Many people ask me this. You don't have to have a book. If you are an expert in a subject, it is really about are you the right person at the right time and can you say the right thing to be on the show? When Oprah's producers are searching for experts, people are naturally and immediately considered an expert if they have written a book, not a self published book, but a book that has been published by a publisher, because that is what is respected in the industry.

One way they begin to search for experts is to look on LexisNexis and on the Dow Jones. These are searchable databases that have all of the articles that have been in print on just about everything forever. When they start to search for experts that is one of the places they look first. They also look at local papers and on television and are very aware of what books are published and who has published it. They are looking at all of these different areas for an expert. Those who have written a book, you are more visible in that way.

If you have been in the media, then you are more visible. If you get local publicity through your local paper, or your local TV shows, those can get the attention of the Oprah producers.

You should have a two-minute video of yourself up on your site that shows you can handle yourself in an interview. The deciding factor between you and another person is having that video up on your site and available. The Oprah producer can go right there, watch your video and make a decision whether you are the kind of guest they want or not.

Jordan: When pitching Oprah, do you suggest calling producers, emailing, or sending a letter in the mail?

Susan: Whatever you are more comfortable with. Some people are more comfortable speaking on the phone. If you have a good ten-second pitch on the phone, then I suggest calling. It is not easy to get through to producers especially if you do not know their direct number or their name. You need to know their name. You can't say I am calling for the producer of the Health Beat or the Celebrity Beat you need to know a producer's name. You can call up and get connected.

The receptionists are becoming more and more protective so it is not as easy to get through anymore. **I recommend that you pitch through the Oprah.com site because they do have people reading all of those pitches every single day**. One of my clients got called back in an hour and another one got called back in five minutes. They really do read them. It is limited to 350 words so you have to be very concise.

In this pitch, you are never going to talk about yourself. It is not about you. It is not about your book, your product, or your cause. It is about the angle and the segment. You are going to say what I envision for the show and why am I the expert to be featured on this particular show. It is not about saying I have this new book or this new product. It is about connecting it to what is happening in the culture today and why it is relevant to Oprah's audience and what does the show look like?

Jordan: In your book you list the names of all the producers and their titles. It is probably a good idea to go on the website because things change so quickly.

Susan: They do not list producers on the website.

Jordan: Right, but you were saying to submit your pitch on line.

Susan: Yes. You can address it to a particular producer through the website. They make sure you are concise by limiting the characters to 2,000 so that is about 350 words. You cannot put any more than that in it.

Jordan: If a producer calls you back, what do you need to know to handle that call well?

Susan: You need to have your notes in front of you about what you want to say. **The most important thing is to first find out what the angle is they are interested in and why they are calling you.** Then you begin to talk to those points and the questions they are asking. Be very specific. This is where you want to be telling stories and showing that you are the best person for their show.

Jordan: If they call back and say, we received your pitch and they want to hear more about it, is it really an audition in a way?

Susan: It is totally an audition. There is no question about it. If you pass the audition, you will go to the next producer, and the next, because it is a series of auditions. It is not just one. It is typically an assistant producer or lower level producer who is calling you for that first audition and that can last anywhere from 5 minutes to 45 minutes. Obviously the longer the better in this particular case, and the more concise you are the better because they are judging you. Are you a good talker? Are you going to be the kind of person who we want on the show? Then you may or may not pass on to that next level.

It is fine to ask, if you have the nerve. If you don't that is fine, but I am the kind of person who would want to know, Do you think that I am one of the candidates that could be on your show or am I not right for you?

Jordan: That is actually a really good tip. I wouldn't think to ask.

Susan: Because otherwise you live in hope. Oh my God. Oprah's producers called and I am going to be on the show, maybe. I would rather know. Not to be hopeful, am I in or am I out? If I am not in, I want to figure out why. That is also one of the qualities of a peak performer. It is about not taking it personally but asking, how could I have performed better, not that it's a performance, but what could I have done differently?

When I am media coaching my clients and we watch their videos together on line,

- What did you think went well?

- What do you think did not go well?
- What would you do differently next time?

It is a process of refining yourself, your pitch, and your audition over time. If you are a great expert in this area and you don't make the cut necessarily that time, it doesn't mean any forever. If they like you and you are a great talker but not quite right for that angle, they will keep you in mind for another angle, if you have the kind of qualities that they are looking for.

Jordan: Even if they decide not to use you, you can ask for their feedback, and then you just got feedback from an Oprah producer.

Susan: Yes. They are not going to tell you at length, you didn't do this right and you didn't do that right, but you will have a sense of what you could improve.

Jordan: Let's say you get on Oprah and you are on the show. I love at the end of your book where you give all the tips about, don't interrupt Oprah, look at Oprah which goes for any TV show. Can you talk about tips while being on the show?

Susan: Yes. **When you are on the show, what you are looking to do is to entertain and enlighten the audience and give a great show.** It is really the most important thing. If you give a great show, then you will be invited back or at least have the potential to be invited back. Other TV show producers will want you too.

The most important thing is to be addressing those questions in a way that is helpful and serves the audience. **You are always thinking about serving the audience first, not serving yourself.** By serving the audience and talking about the subject matter that is informative and enlightening, you will automatically create desire in the audience to want what you have. Part of that is to be very fluent and natural and vulnerable particularly on Oprah.

I remember teaching at one of the Learning Annexes and one person raised their hand and they said, "Susan, you said you want to see natural and vulnerable and yet you are telling us there are all these things that we can and can't do on TV. How are we supposed to be able to do both? How can we be natural when we have to be trained in all these different areas?"

One of the things that is very important to get on Oprah and be comfortable on Oprah is to practice on camera. **People are really judging you and understanding you in less than four seconds. It is all about body language and facial language**. It is not about your verbal language. **The most important thing on television is to feel comfortable in your body** and to be at ease because it conveys everything.

Of course you must have your words in order but that is really secondary. One of the things to do and to understand is to be able to look at the host or whoever is talking 100 percent of the time with your eyes. Be able to give a neutral interested look and BE actually interested and engaged.

I had one client who is very famous, so I can't mention his name, but he had the opposite problem because he was so canned and so rehearsed. I thought oh my God, I have heard these answers a million times and you could tell that he was not engaged by the kind of answers that he gave. That is the opposite extreme of being a great guest.

There was another guest on the show who was really present and it was very apparent that he was completely engaged. In order to be engaged, you need to be relaxed. In order to be relaxed, you need to have the experience of being in that kind of environment quite a lot of times so you can relax, enjoy yourself and be in the moment.

Jordan: It is very important to have some media training. How does someone find a good media trainer? Maybe they don't know where to look or maybe they don't know what to look for.

Susan: A lot of people are not ready for media training. Of course, I am a media trainer and I do it on the phone for people all over the world and you can also get lots of great experience on your own by getting interviewed by your friends on camera. Then watch yourself and start to iron out those things that will be pretty obvious to you on camera. Most people are pretty perceptive about what they do not like about themselves. We are all a little bit harsh with ourselves.

I remember a woman I interviewed for *Sell Yourself Without Selling Your Soul* when we were doing on-camera media coaching. She started yelling at the camera saying, "Well look at that. Look at that woman. She is lying. Who would believe her? What does she know?" She was talking about herself. I said, "Let's talk about all the things you don't like about yourself first and then why do you think this woman is lying?"

- It is about being able to look at yourself in an objective manner.
- Get used to having a camera trained on you
- Get comfortable with speaking in 15-second sound bytes back and forth with a friend of yours before you ever get on a local TV show.

Jordan: For people listening, your website is www.OprahPRSecrets.com.

Susan: www.OprahPRSecrets.com

On the website, for people who are not yet ready for Oprah or to get the Oprah kit and the O book, there are plenty of free things on my site. There is my newsletter, which comes out once a month. There are also free teleclasses that you can download. There are lots of free things to do if you are not yet ready to move forward with Oprah. After this kind of conversation and those of you who are willing to move on with Oprah, we have the special for these two days.

Jordan: Do you have any idea how Oprah's favorite things are selected?

Susan: For the show?

Jordan: Right. Is it really Oprah's favorite things or do people pitch products to the show?

Susan: They do pitch products to the show. Oftentimes these products are sent in to the show and then the staff will test them. It goes through this whole process, part of which is a secret, because the process is a secret. This isn't so much of a pitch as it is about a product, do they love the product or not? Are these things that are going to be of interest to women? People send in their products and then the staff tests them. Many times it may be after a series of products are sent in and each time you do a different pitch. It may be a number of times that product is pitched. Is there a process for it because these are physical objects? They are naturally sent in.

This one woman had a company called Let's Take the Cake. She sent in her cake   and it was a Key Lime Bundt cake and they really loved the cake. It has to be very beautiful and be able to translate on the air as something beautifully packaged. You have to be able to ship it and have those products in stock in order to be able to satisfy that kind of demand. It is this 'behind the scenes' type of booking people, they review it as a team and then it is over a period of time that these are selected. Does that make sense?

Jordan: It does. Would you recommend sending it to producers?

Susan: Yes, you send it to producers. Everything should be sent to a producer, never to Oprah directly. I do want to mention that the producers are the ones that you should be thanking. Yes it is lovely to give Oprah a gift after you have been on the show, but really the producers are doing the hard work so please send them a gift and a thank you.

Jordan: Right. It looks like our time is almost up and I want to go over the offer that you have made to people on the call. I will go over it and you can clarify anything that you want. They are going to get the Ultimate Oprah kit, which includes CDs and your book, *The Ultimate Guide to Getting Booked on Oprah* and *How to get in O Magazine*, those are the two products right?

Susan: Yes.

Jordan: The CD's, the book, and the O Magazine. Usually it is $344.00 but if you order before Friday at midnight, this Friday at midnight, we are taking $100.00 off so it is just $244.00. I will send you an email but it is www.snipurl/1i4an. If you hear this later you can go to www.AppearOnOprah.com. Thank you again, Susan. This is a lot of great information.

Susan: Thank you. I hope all of you feel inspired to move toward getting on Oprah. Please keep me posted when you get that call from the producer and get on the show. I would love to hear from you.

Jordan: Susan's website is www.OprahPRSecrets.com. You can give her feedback, contact her about media training or subscribe to her free newsletter. Thanks so much and I will talk to you guys later.

ADDITIONAL RESOURCES:

Appear On Oprah
www.AppearOnOprah.com

Appear In O Magazine
www.AppearInOMagazine.com

Oprah PR Secrets
www.OprahPRSecrets.com

RECOMMENDED RESOURCES:

Celebrity Black Book
www.CelebrityBlackBook.com

Celebrity Book Endorsements Toolkit
www.BookEndorsements.com

Celebrity Causes Database
www.CelebCauses.com

Celebrity Fundraising Success
www.CelebrityFundraising.com

Celebrity Leverage Secrets
www.CelebrityLeverage.com

Secrets To Contacting Celebrities
www.SecretsToContactingCelebrities.com

Notes:

Notes:

Notes:

Notes:

Notes: